D1532980

1

THE IMAGE OF MARY

THE IMAGE OF

MARY

ACCORDING TO THE EVANGELISTS

HORACIO BOJORGE, S.J.
Translated by Aloysius Owen, S.J.

ALBA · HOUSE   NEW · YORK

SOCIETY OF ST. PAUL, 2187 VICTORY BLVD., STATEN ISLAND, NEW YORK 10314

Library of Congress Cataloging in Publication Data

Bojorge, Horacio.
The image of Mary according to the Evangelists.

1. Mary, Virgin--Biblical teaching. I. Title.
BT611.B64   232.91   77-15516
ISBN 0-8189-0362-7

Nihil Obstat:
Daniel V. Flynn, J.C.D.
Censor Librorum

Imprimatur:
✝*James P. Mahoney, D.D.*
Vicar General, Archdiocese of New York
November 27, 1977

Produced in the United States of
America by the Fathers and Brothers of the
Society of St. Paul, 2187 Victory Boulevard,
Staten Island, New York, 10314, as part of their
communications apostolate.

3 4 5 6 7 8 9 (Current Printing: first digit).

TABLE OF CONTENTS

INTRODUCTION:

MARY IN THE NEW TESTAMENT

It is remarkable that, when we look in the New Testament for what is said about the Most Blessed Virgin Mary, out of the 27 books which make up the canon of the New Testament only four mention Mary by name, while one speaks of her only as the *Mother of Jesus* or *His Mother* but *never mentions her by name*. The four are the gospels of Matthew, Mark and Luke and the book of The Acts of the Apostles. None of the remaining 22 books speak to us directly about Mary. It is only through the eyes of faith that we attribute to her the role she plays in certain passages; for instance, where it is said Jesus is the Son of David, or that we are children of the Promise, or of the heavenly Jerusalem, or that the Father sent His Son, born of a woman, or where there is found the mysterious woman crowned with stars in the Book of Revelation.

If we rely on our first impression, it seems that Mary, who is explicitly mentioned in only 5 books out of 27, has been acknowledged by only one half of the inspired writers of the New Testament. Matthew, Mark, Luke, John and Paul are the only ones who speak of her, and, in fact, Paul only mentions her once in Gal 4:4-5. James, Peter and Jude do not mention her at all.

Consequently, to speak of Mary's image in the New Testament is to speak of Mary seen through Matthew, Mark, Luke and John, that is, through *the evangelists*.

Notice we do not say *"through the gospels"* but *"through the evangelists."* We might have used the first phrase had not the evangelist Luke spoken of her outside of his gospel in the Acts of the Apostles 1:14, and had not John in the Book of Revelation spoken of her as a woman, now identified with the Church.

Mary in the New Testament is practically Mary in the Gospels. This is so because outside of the gospels practically nothing is said about Mary.

Two approaches may be taken for contemplating Mary's image as seen through the gospels: one *synthetic*, the other *analytic*. The former consists in synthesizing the various data found in the four gospels and thus forming a single image of Mary: the tracing of one single portrait, the result of combining four distinct descriptions. The analytic approach, the one we have adopted, consists in considering separately the four images or likenesses of Mary.

The synthetic approach may more appropriately be called: The image of Mary seen in the gospels. The analytic approach is that of *The image*, or more appropriately, *the images of Mary seen through the evangelists*, the title we have chosen.

We all know, of course, that there is only one gospel, that of our Lord Jesus Christ. Yet the same God who willed that there be one sole message of salvation, also willed that four presentations of that message be handed down to us. This gospel is quadriform, as St. Irenaeus observed long ago in refutation of the errors of heretics who pitted what one evangelist said against what was said by another (*Adv. Haereses* III, 11).

This quadriform presentation of the gospel is what gives us the depth, the perspective and the projection of converging views. Thereby we see one single view of Jesus, hear one single voice of Jesus, one only Jesus and one only salvific work of Jesus yet in four perspectives and four ways of presentation. Each one of the evangelists has his own peculiar manner of depicting the image of Jesus, and all that each one of them says serves for fashioning this portrait of Jesus they draw for us.

Should we be surprised that, consequently, this quadriform presentation selects historical truths, narrates events, at times changes the chronological order, so that it may follow its own theological logic (Pardon the redundancy!) and subordinates the manner of presentation of events and persons to the end of effectively showing Jesus and His message according to His divine inspiration and the circumstances of time, place and person? Should we be surprised that the diverse aspects employed by the four evangelists for narrating the same events and presenting the same and sole person of Jesus, allow of their giving us four distinct presentations of Mary?

Granted that the mystery of Mary is an aspect of the Mystery of Christ, every permissible change of approaching the mystery of Christ (which as a divine mystery is by definition susceptible of an inexhaustible number of diverse approaches—though they can never be contradictory—), brings along with it corresponding changes of approach in the mystery of Mary.

There is one Jesus Christ presented in four ways and one mystery of Mary presented in four ways. Besides there is a very special and significant coherence between the way each evangelist shows us Jesus and in the way each one shows us Mary, consonant with his own peculiar presentation of Jesus.

Let us now be guided by the evangelists, one after the other. Let us try to penetrate each one's understanding of the Lord through his manner of presenting to us the image of Mary. The maxim: "To Jesus through Mary" is not a modern invention, without roots in the two-thousand-year-old tradition of our Holy Mother the Church. It is already rooted in the gospels, and in so far as we can trace their use of it, is found in an oral tradition prior to them, a tradition from which they drew their written formulations. Let us, then, allow the evangelists to bring us through Mary to a greater knowledge of *the Lord who is coming and for whom we are waiting.*

THE IMAGE OF MARY

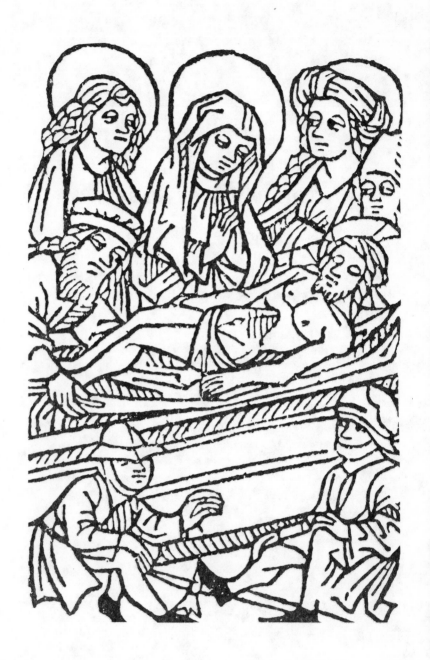

I

THE IMAGE OF MARY AS SEEN THROUGH ST. MARK

THE EARLIEST IMAGE

We begin with Mark, whose gospel is the shortest and almost certainly the earliest of the four gospels. It is the one which most likely brings together the religious teaching and preaching of St. Peter, or, we may say, the gospel according to the way Peter proclaimed it.

In regard to Mary this gospel of St. Mark is extremely reticent, comparable, by its paucity of references, to the great Marian silence of the New Testament. Mark begins his gospel by presenting the figure of St. John the Baptist and, almost immediately thereafter, that of Jesus, already grown to manhood, who comes to be baptized in the Jordan. In his gospel he does not give any account of Jesus' infancy, unlike Matthew and Luke whose accounts tell us something about His Mother. Nor is there in Mark's gospel anything comparable to the two grand scenes in the gospel according to St. John: the marriage feast of Cana, and Calvary.

1. *Two texts:* Mk 3:31-35; 6:1-3

Two very brief passages cover all that Mark tells us about Mary, both found in the first part of his gospel. He is quite impersonal, maintaining the cold objectivity of a chronicler, and lets us know what third parties say about Mary. Analyzing the text we find that these third parties are unbelievers, enemies of Jesus. Of course, they do not look kindly on His Mother but

include her in their hostility and disbelief. What Jesus says about
Mary in these passages is due to this hostility and disbelief and is
intended to confound and refute them.

Let us quote these passages from the gospel of St. Mark:

> His mother and his brothers arrived, and as they stood outside
> they sent word to him to come out. The crowd seated around
> him told him: "Your mother and your brothers and sisters are
> outside asking for you." He said in reply: "Who are my mother
> and my brothers?" And gazing around him at those seated in
> the circle he continued: "These are my mother and my broth-
> ers. Whoever does the will of God is brother and sister and
> mother to me" (Mk 3:31-35).

> He departed from there and returned to his own part of
> the country followed by his disciples. When the sabbath came
> he began to teach in the synagogue in a way that kept his large
> audience amazed. They said: "Where did he get all this? What
> kind of wisdom is he endowed with? How is it that such
> miraculous deeds are accomplished by his hands? Is this not
> the carpenter, the son of Mary, a brother of James and Joses
> and Judas and Simon? Are not his sisters our neighbors here?"
> They found him too much for them (Mk 6:1-3).

Here we find the skeptical outcry of those who were amazed
and did not believe in his inexplicable power and wisdom.

These two passages are the only ones in Mark's gospel which
mention Mary. They simply prove that Jesus was known as the
carpenter, the Son of Mary. They also show that this sonship
made it more unbelievable for many that He was sent by God.
It served as an excuse for those ill-disposed to maintain their
disbelief. For the very sublimity of the manifestations of power
and wisdom—as Mark relates—which Jesus was going about giving everywhere, was a proof that they did not derive from a human heritage or source, but were a gift from on high. The same
lowliness of His Galilean parentage—the region proverbially most
ignorant of the law among the Jewish people—must have been a

convincing proof of the divine origin of His works. If they were inexplicable through the flesh and parentage, would not the explanation have to be found in the Spirit of God?

2. The context of the gospel

Now, however, let us try to understand better the meaning of these episodes, placing them in the perspective of Mark's account. The whole first part of his gospel, up to chapter 8, verses 27-30—Peter's profession—shows us a Jesus who works marvels and portents, who arouses the admiration of the people, who dazzles them by His superhuman power. That is, it shows us the progressive and growing revelation of Jesus. At the same time, it shows us the absolute and general incomprehension of the true nature of His person and His mission. Jesus reveals Himself, but no one understands His revelation. Those who do not believe in Him do not understand it, nor do those who dispute with Him, nor those to whom He speaks in parables.

This lack of understanding on the part of unbelievers is not surprising. What is surprising is that neither do His own disciples understand Him. In Peter's privileged profession, which concludes the first part of the gospel, there is glimpsed an abysmal ignorance of and a stubborn resistance to the sorrowful aspect of the identity of Jesus the Messiah.

Just a short while before Jesus began His career on a Sabbath at Capernaum, teaching in the synagogue and healing many infirm and expelling demons. A short while before, too, His first disciples began to follow Him and popular enthusiasm grew. At the same time, at the very beginning of His career, opposition started and He was severely criticized. They charged Him with curing on the Sabbath, eating with sinners, allowing His disciples to pluck grain-heads on the Sabbath. As early as the beginning of the third chapter, the Pharisees conspired with the Herodians to see how they might get rid of Him. This is hard to do because large throngs followed Jesus. He chooses from among them His numerous disciples. One of the first steps of the conspiracy is mentioned in 3:20-21. Jesus returns to His own country. Once again the crowd will be there with not enough to eat.

When His family heard of this, they came to take charge of Him, saying: "He is out of His mind" (Mk 3:21).

3. *Antagonism toward the Messiah*

The first move by the conspirators against Jesus is to declare that He is mad and to induce His relatives to restrain Him. They were warned that their kinsman might well implicate them in His follies and cause them some problems. Such intimidation of relatives, as in this instance, was a common practice as shown by the episode of the man born blind in St. John's gospel, when his parents were summoned to testify before the tribunal (Jn 9: 18-23).

When Jesus' relatives heard that He was said to be mad, and perhaps since they were moved by fears and veiled threats, they hastened to restrain Him. They made His Mother come with them, hoping Jesus would not be able to resist her pleas. Meanwhile Mark records the crescendo of accusations leveled against Jesus. Now He is not merely charged with being mad, but as possessed by the devil, "possessed by Beelzebub" (Mk 3:22).

In the midst of this tempest of hostility, on the one hand, and of popular enthusiasm, on the other, as Mark, laconically as a chronicler, relates: "His mother and his brothers arrived, and as they stood outside they sent word to him to come out."

A family problem is to be settled. The lowly Galilean townsfolk do not want to discuss theological matters. Out of humility, modesty or peasant prudence—for lack of a formal education does not mean stupidity—they do not go in. (Or, as Luke says, the crowd would not let them pass through): "There was a large crowd seated around him."

The despised teacher is surrounded by an enthusiastic audience which felt their hearts enflamed by His words. "They were spellbound by his teaching because he taught with authority and not like the scribes" (Mk 1:22). A malicious person, who had sneaked in with the others, shouted at Jesus: "Listen! Your mother, your brothers and your sisters are outside asking for you." He says this to Jesus, but indirectly he intends to bring to the attention of the audience from what kind of a family their teacher has come! Further on, in the sixth chapter, Mark records that these seeds of malice had taken root: " 'Is this not the carpenter, the son of Mary, a brother of James and Joses and Judas and Simon? Are not his sisters our neighbors here?' They found him too much for them" (Mk 6:3).

Mary's lowly background and that of Jesus' relatives is wielded to humiliate Him before His hearers: "This is one who claims to be a King and a Messiah?" "This is a teacher and a savior?" "Here is one from whom was born a prophet?" This is precisely the objection St. John tells us about: "At this the Jews started to murmur in protest because He claimed: 'I am the bread that came down from heaven.' They kept saying: 'Is this not Jesus, the son of Joseph? Do we not know his father and mother? How can he claim to have come down from heaven?' " (Jn 6:42). John then records, too, that many of His disciples "broke away and would not remain in His company any longer." They said: "This sort of talk is hard to endure!" (Jn 6:60, 66).

John also tells us: "As a matter of fact, not even his brothers had much confidence in him" (Jn 7:5). As for the Jews he says: "The Jews were filled with amazement and said: 'How did this man get his education when he had no teacher?' " (Jn 7:15).

Mark makes us hear those who speak of Mary, Jesus' mother, out of their deep hostility toward her Son. In their words there is stress on the lowly human origins of Jesus, which is a tacit denial of His divine origin and character.

Just as there will be an *"Ecce homo!"* which mocks Jesus in His passion, there too is a preview which covers Mary with the same insults and contempt: *"Ecce mulier! Ecce Mater ejus!"* "Behold the man!" "Behold the woman! Behold His Mother!"

4. The testimony of Jesus

In response to this hostility, hypocritically concealed under the courtesy of announcing the presence of his relatives who were outside, Jesus replied by asking a controversial question: "Who are my mother and my brothers?" and by giving an equally controversial answer to His question: "And gazing around him at those seated in the circle he continued: 'These are my mother and my brothers. Whoever does the will of God is brother and sister and mother to me'."

The gospels say that Jesus often calls His disciples His brothers, those who hear Him with faith, although they do not understand Him perfectly. There are those who do not oppose Him, but follow and listen to Him. This is Jesus' family, because it is the Father's family. Its family bond is not simply blood, but the New Covenant is the Blood of Jesus, that is, belief in Him.

As St. John explains: "Any who did accept him, he empowered to become children of God" (Jn 1:12). That is why Jesus concludes with an explanation of why these are His true relatives: "Whoever does the will of God is brother and sister and mother to me." In the text by Luke we have: "My mother and my brothers are those who hear the word of God and act upon it" (Lk 8:21). The mysterious and for many the not quite evident sameness between "doing the will of God" and believing in Jesus Christ, is shown to us explicitly in John's First Epistle: ". . . we are keeping his commandments and doing what is pleasing in his sight. His commandment is this: we are to believe in the name of his Son, Jesus Christ, and are to love one another as he commanded us" (1 Jn 3:22-23).

Doing the will of the Father is not to bow down to an obscure wish, but is to find pleasure in doing what pleases God and rejoice in God's joy. If we are asked what pleases and gives joy to our God, who as an omnipotent Being may seem hard to please, we know the answer because this inaccessible Being has revealed to us in what He finds joy: "This is my beloved. Listen to him" (Mk 9:7); "This is my beloved Son on whom my favor rests. Listen to him" (Mt 17:5); "This is my Son, my Chosen One. Listen to him" (Lk 9:35). Our God reveals Himself as the

Father who loves His Son, Jesus Christ, and delights in Him, and asks nothing else of us except that we listen to Him filled with faith, and follow Him as His disciples.

Now, perhaps, we understand why Luke translates "doing the will of God" as found in Matthew and Mark by the equivalent expression "Listen to His Word," that is, "Listen to His Son" and "Keep it," that is, "Follow Him as a disciple." There is also a passage in St. John's gospel which brings out this identity between the Word of Jesus and the will of God: "My doctrine is not my own; it comes from him who sent me. Any man who chooses to do his will, will know about this doctrine—namely, whether it comes from God or is simply spoken on my own" (Jn 7:16-17). They, then, are relatives of Jesus who through belief in Him are linked by the bond of compliance which unites the Father with the Son and the Son with the Father.

Therefore, His response to those who vilify Him along with His Mother is a serious warning. It is equivalent to His setting Himself apart from them and denying them any other possibility of entering into communion with God, except through belief in Him. Yet there is another aspect to these words of Jesus. It is one of praise, of a declaration of a Covenant of relationship, a relationship which is the only real and true one between the believer and Him and much stronger than that of blood. In so far as Mary merited to be His Mother by having believed, this is the highest and worthiest testimony Mark could have given us about Mary. It is the testimony of Jesus as to the ultimate and sole reason why Mary could come to be His Mother: faith in Him.

5. Mary, Mother of Jesus through faith

Mary was not united to Jesus only or primarily by the bond of blood. That this bond could come about, she had to have had prior to this a bond which Jesus esteems as much more important.

Mark does not explicitly state all this. Nor undoubtedly did Jesus do so on this occasion. We have come to understand by other ways what is implied in the veiled testimony of Jesus which Mark relates, namely, that Mary believed in Jesus before Jesus was Jesus; that only because the Word found in her such faith as this, could He become flesh.

So, in this way Mark's Marian silence is broken by the Marian eloquence of Jesus Himself. It is an eloquence which bears the stamp of authenticity by its very enigmatic style, veiled and in parables, the style Jesus used in all His polemics, in a language that is revelation for the believer, but obscurity for the unbeliever.

I want to conclude—in confirmation of what has been said—by shedding light on this first image of Mary according to Mark. The light will come from Luke's gospel, yet we can be quite sure it shone not only from his pen but from the same pre-evangelical tradition on which Mark relies. I like to regard the incident recounted in Luke as the same as that reported in Mark, due to the similarities found in the texts. At the very moment Jesus was being accused of being possessed by the devil, and was defending Himself: "While he was saying this a woman from the crowd called out, 'Blest is the womb that bore you and the breasts that nursed you!' 'Rather,' he replied, 'blest are they who hear the word of God and keep it' " (Lk 11:27-28).

I think that Luke, when he inserted this episode in his gospel, intended to express discretely what he judged Mark did not adequately express, namely, that the words of Jesus in response to those who told Him His relatives had arrived, contained a testimony to Mary.

Conclusion

The image of Mary seen through Mark is, in comparison with that seen through Matthew and Luke, the most primitive image we can trace through the writings of the New Testament. It is of the pre-evangelical tradition and goes back to Jesus Himself.

Though it is a lightly-sketched image, it still is clear in its essential traits. We shall see these traits as the other evangelists will develop and express them, confining ourselves, however, to show only what was already implied in the image of Mary, the unknown mother of an unknown Messiah, a vilified mother of one who was vilified. Yet, for Jesus, blessed because of her faith in Him. A mother through faith almost more so than through her blood.

From the very beginning and from the very testimony of Jesus: mother of the Messiah, presented, in express relationship with those who believe in Jesus, as mother of His disciples, that is, mother of His Church.

II

THE IMAGE OF MARY AS SEEN THROUGH ST. MATTHEW

THE ORIGIN OF THE MESSIAH

1. *From Mark to Matthew*

Mark, whose image of Mary we have just seen, wrote his gospel for the Christian community of Rome, intending particularly to explain an event the Jews of the diaspora in that city asked Christian missioners to explain. They wanted to know: how was it possible that, if Jesus was the Son of God and the Messiah, He was not acknowledged, was rejected and condemned to death by the leaders of Palestine? Mark's entire gospel shows us, on the one hand, the revelation of Jesus as Messiah, as the Christ or as the Anointed, all three titles having exactly the same meaning, while, on the other hand, he shows us the progressive disbelief of many, the misunderstanding, even by His own believers, of the suffering He was to undergo as Messiah. The sketchy image of Mary drawn by Mark—as we have seen it—is linked to this perspective in his gospel. He shows us one of the ways Jesus was rejected and opposed by the Palestinian leaders and how they introduced in their campaign of defamation and persecution the lowly condition and Galilean origin of His family.

In the face of this antagonism, Jesus responds—fearlessly—to those who ask for a genealogical sign, confronting them with the necessity of believing without asking for a sign, and giving a testimony—obscure to unbelievers, but eloquent for those who believed in Him—favorable to His Mother and to His disciples.

Matthew, of whose image of Mary we shall now treat, is acquainted with Mark's image. He retouches it in his gospel (Mt 12:46-50; 13:53-57) as does St. Luke in his (Lk 8:19-21; 4:22). There is no need to go over these passages which are almost a textual copy of Mark or of a pre-existing source, since Matthew only introduces some slight retouches. We are going to concern ourselves with what he has garnered for enhancing Mary's image, namely, what will make explicit what is implied in Mark.

2. Mary, Virgin and Spouse of Joseph

Matthew embellishes Mary's image as compared to that of Mark. He explains two characteristics of the Mother of the Messiah: 1) Mary is a Virgin; 2) Mary is the spouse of Joseph, son of David. Matthew explains both characteristics not in order to satisfy curiosity, but in order to bring out their meaning in the framework of his theological presentation of the mysterious origin of the Messiah.

Mary's virginity is a Marian characteristic which is in intimate relationship with the *divine* sonship and origin of the Messiah. He is born of Mary without any intervention of man and by the operation of the Holy Spirit, as Matthew says.

That Mary is the Spouse of Joseph, Son of David, is a Marian characteristic which is in turn in intimate connection with the Davidic sonship and human character of the Messiah.

Son of God, by the mystery of His Mother's virginity, and *Son of David* by the no less mysterious marriage with Joseph, Son of David.

3. *The human-divine origin of the Messiah. Son of David born of a woman*

Innumerable Christian painters have portrayed the Mother and Child. We think Matthew is the precursor and pioneer of this extensive gallery. None the less, the earliest text we have of Jesus and His Mother most probably is that of St. Paul. The very minimal Mariological image of St. Paul merits here our attention, even though it be but in passing. Around the year A.D. 51, or some twenty years before the probable date of the composition of Matthew's gospel, Paul writes to the Galatians: "But when the designated time had come, *God sent forth his Son born of a woman*, born under law, to deliver from the law those who were subjected to it, so that they might receive our status as adopted sons" (Gal 4:4-5).

Some ten or twelve years later, A.D. 61 or 63, Paul, during his first imprisonment, writes to the faithful in Rome: "Greetings from Paul, a servant of Christ Jesus, called to be an apostle and set apart to proclaim the gospel of God which he promised long ago through his prophets, as the Holy Scriptures record—the gospel concerning his Son, who was descended from David according to the flesh but was made Son of God in power according to the spirit of holiness . . ." (Rm 1:1-3).

Both these texts of Paul show us the presence in the most primitive state of the tradition, of three essential elements we are going to find in the Marian passages of Matthew.

The first is that what is said of Jesus Christ is presented as having happened *according to Scripture*, as fulfilling Scripture, as the realization of what was foretold by the prophets who spoke in God's name and were enlightened by the Holy Spirit.

The second is the *two-fold Sonship* of Jesus: Son of God and at the same time Son of David. Paul sees in Jesus two sonships: one spiritual by which He is Son of God by operation of the Spirit which permits us to cry out: "Abba!", Father; the other, a sonship according to the flesh by which He is Son of David.

The third is that it is to be noted that it is not specified how this Davidic descent comes about by saying: "engendered by Joseph" or "born of man" but by telling us "Born of a woman."* Here are the constituent elements of one of the problems Matthew will answer in his gospel. It is the same problem that is discussed in the texts of Mark which we have already seen. But now it is no longer posed in terms of an objection, in the mouths of enemies, but in terms of a reply to their objections. It is a response which doubtless is inspired by the response Jesus Himself had given in the times of His mortal flesh and which the three synoptics relate to us in their gospels (Mt 22:41ff. and its parallels).

We shall quote the texts: "In turn Jesus put a question to the assembled Pharisees, 'What is your opinion about the Messiah? Whose son is he?' 'David's,' they answered. He said to them, 'Then how is it that David under the Spirit's influence calls him 'lord,' as he does: 'The Lord said to my Lord, Sit at my right hand, until I humble your enemies beneath your feet'? If David calls him 'lord', how can he be his son?' No one could give him an answer; therefore no one dared, from that day on, to ask him any questions" (Mt 22:41ff). The text in the above passage from the Old Testament is from Ps 110:1.

Jesus had now alerted His hearers to the danger of judging Him exclusively *according to the flesh.* Not that He rejected the Davidic origin of the Messiah, but rather He pointed out that this Davidic origin involved a mystery, and that the mystery of the personality of the Messiah was not to be understood exclusively by His Davidic origin but by a root which made Him superior to His ancestors according to the flesh, and which opened up room in the mystery of His origin for divine intervention, for "Lord" was a title reserved for God.

---

*Translator's note, apropos of note in text. We have followed the text of the Jerusalem Bible. To justify "made of a woman" instead of "born" the reader may consult the article by Jose M. Bover, S.J., *Un texto de San Pablo* (Gal 4:4-5) *interpretado por San Ireneo* (*Estudios Eclesiasticos* XVII [1943] 145-181), the translation used by the author.

It is in this twofold, complex sonship of the Messiah, in the convergence of these two titles: Son of God and Son of David, that Matthew sets the mystery of Mary.

4. The revelation of Mary's virginity

Matthew concludes his genealogy of Jesus thus: "Jacob was the father of Joseph, the husband of Mary. It was of her that Jesus who is called the Messiah was born" (Mt 16). The formula is interesting. Throughout the entire genealogy with which Matthem begins his gospel he uses the expression "father of:" "Abraham was the father of Isaac, Isaac the father of Jacob." When, counter to Hebraic genealogical custom, he mentions a mother, he says: "Judah was the father of Perez and Zerah, *whose mother was Tamar*," "David was the father of Solomon, *whose mother* had been the wife of Uriah. . . Jacob was the father of Joseph, the husband of Mary."

Joseph is the last of whom he speaks as "*fathered*." He does not now say: "*Joseph was the father of Jesus whose mother was Mary*" but "*Joseph was the husband of Mary. It was of her that Jesus who is called the Messiah was born*." Thereby Matthew poses a problem for a Jewish reader who is conversant with Hebraic genealogy. He will answer this problem in some subsequent verses: "Now this is how the birth of Jesus Christ came about. When his mother Mary was engaged to Joseph, but before they lived together, she was found to be with child through the power of the Holy Spirit."

Here we have the revelation of Mary's virginity. We are amazed that this is said so calmly, so unemotionally by Matthew about so marvelous a portent. He does not stress it, nor does he try to impress us, nor does he attempt to bring out its significance; he merely states it as a matter of fact. He is more concerned about the theological meaning than about its extraordinary singularity. He is more concerned about the problem of interpretation which confronted Joseph the Just than with that which may confront all generations of man after him. Theologi-

cally, then, what is the significance of the virginal maternity of
Mary?

Matthew is not concerned here with giving arguments to
make it credible or acceptable. There is no reason to think his
contemporaries were more credulous than our own nor more
inclined to accept without ridicule this mystery of a virgin
mother. We have seen the objections they brought up against
a Jesus said to be the carnal son of Joseph and Mary. Imagine
the objections which could have been brought up against someone who should present himself—or be presented—under the pre-
tension of being the Son of a Virgin Mother, of having been
engendered without the participation of a man but by a direct
operation of God in the womb of His mother.

5. Genealogy

We shall now consider the role played by genealogical litera-
ture in the life of the Jewish people in the time of Jesus. Thereby
we shall better understand the aim of Matthew's interest in the
virginal conception of Jesus and His adoption by Joseph taking
Mary for his wife, and why he sets this gem in the context—not
too attractive for us—of a genealogy.

In Jesus' time, the genealogy of a person and of a family was
of the highest juridical importance and implied serious consequences in the social and religious life. It was not, as today among
us, a matter of historical curiosity, or of pompousness, or of a
mere satisfaction of vanity. A genealogy was preserved as a family title. On it depended social position, and racial and religious
origin. Only those families which preserved the purity of origin
of the Chosen People formed part of the *true Israel*, such as it
had been established, after the Exile, by the religious reformation
of Esdras.

Every dignity, every office of trust, every important public
charge, was reserved for the *pure* Israelites. Their purity had to
be proven and the Sanhedrin relied on a tribunal charged with
investigating the origins of aspirants to these offices.

The most important privilege which a pure genealogy brought was in the *strictly* religious domain. Thanks to purity of origin the Israelite participated in the merits of his ancestors. Above all, every Israelite shared, by virtue of descent from Abraham, the merits of the Patriarch and partook of the promises God made to Abraham. For instance, every Israelite had the right to be heard in prayer, to be protected from danger, helped in warfare, pardoned for his sins, saved from Gehenna and be admitted into the Kingdom of God. Literally, the Kingdom of God was acquired by inheritance. Jesus vigorously opposed this belief. This is as clear as crystal from the following texts. "Do not begin by saying to yourselves, 'Abraham is our father.' I tell you, God can raise up children to Abraham from these stones" (Lk 3:8); "Let me make it clear that tax collectors and prostitutes are entering the kingdom of God before you." Jesus is telling them that the title to enter the Kingdom of Heaven is not genealogical purity, but faith (Cf. Jn 3:3ff; 8:33ff.).

6. Son of David

Yet, besides, and secondarily, the purity of a genealogical line gave the descendant a share in the particular merits of his own ancestors. A descendant of David, for instance, shared in David's merits and was especially accredited with the divine promises made to David. That is why, when Matthew begins his gospel with the genealogical origin of the Messiah, he starts out with a point of greatest import for every Jew of his times, the Davidic origin of the Messiah.

According to the common, current conviction of Jesus' contemporaries, the Messiah, based on Scripture, would be a descendant of David. In the Palestine of Jesus' time, in addition to the Sons of Levi, there were other groups, families or clans, which bore the names of illustrious ancestors. There existed a whole clan of David's descendants—one of whom was Joseph—which must have been very numerous, not only in Bethlehem, the city of David's origin, but also in Jerusalem and throughout Palestine.

It is no exaggeration to say that the number of David's Sons was at least some one or two thousand. To be a son of David, was then to bear a current name, which did not necessarily give the bearer too much pomp and glory. In fact, we might compare it to the patronymics of today: Johnson, Fitzpatrick, Ivanovich, Lopez, etc.

In the gospel Jesus' near relatives appear to be a numerous group, and it seems that they were an important nucleus in Jerusalem, perhaps around a hundred. Among the Sons of David there were doubtless, poor and well-off families. Doubtless, too, some were members of the aristocracy of Jerusalem. The glamor, the popularity, and the success of Jesus' claim to be the Messiah could not but incite feelings of envy among the more wealthy and illustrious Sons of David. This would be especially so in as much as it would frustrate the hope of divine election held by more than one Davidic mother proud of her sons, with more titles, relations and learning than those in Galilee.

Matthew's assertion of the Davidic origin of Joseph deserves to be wholly believed. It is not a later invention of the New Testament intended to supply a foundation for the Messianic origin of Jesus by making Him a descendant of David. This is abundantly clear from the unanimous testimony of the entire New Testament and that of other historical sources. Eusebius records in his *Ecclesiastical History* Hegesipus' testimony, written around 180 A.D., about a Palestinian tradition that the nephews of Jude, the Lord's brother, were denounced to Domitian as descendants of David and they admitted before his tribunal their Davidic origin.

Likewise Simon, the Lord's cousin and the successor of James in the government of the community of Jerusalem, was denounced as a Son of David and of Messianic descent and for this was crucified. Julius Africanus confirms that Jesus' relatives took pride in their Davidic origin. All this leads to the conclusion that not even the most virulent opponents of Jesus questioned His Davidic origin. Had they done so it would have been a powerful argument against Him, an allegation which could have been made before the people.

For Matthew everything would have been at first sight more simple had he been able to present Jesus as a son of Joseph, His father, as all His ancestors were mentioned as sons of their fathers. Actually, Jesus' virginal birth complicates matters for him. It not only introduces into his account a real stumbling block, a scandal for many, but also complicates the evidence of Jesus' Davidic origin by transposing it from the physical level to that of the legal bonds of adoption.

What is the theological meaning of the title *Son of David*—a title commonly used—applied to the Messiah? How does Matthew understand it as a title applicable to Jesus?

Matthew's gospel starts out thus: "A family record of Jesus Christ, son of David, son of Abraham." He uses Messianic titles which are most common and accepted. This he does in order to show to what extent they are false and to what extent they are true. He does this intending to show that it is not the titles which enlighten us about the Messiah's identity, but it is the Messiah-Jesus and His life which teach us their real meaning.

As Son of David, Jesus is the bearer of the promises made to David *for Israel*. As Son of Abraham, He brings the promise *to all peoples*. As Son of David, He is King, but a king rejected and persecuted even unto death from His cradle, for at His birth Herod, fearing his reign threatened by His mere existence, orders the slaughter of the Innocents. It is not the sages of His people but those of the pagans, having come from the East, who seek the king of the Jews and bear Him gifts. As Son of David, He is to be born in Bethlehem, but His origin is not known, for He is called a Nazarene of Galilee.

The meaning of this initial recognition of the titles: *Son of David, Son of Abraham,* is made clear by the final term of the genealogy: Son of Mary (by the working of the Holy Spirit), wife of Joseph.

Mary and Joseph, concluding the genealogical list, cast on it a light that transfigures it. The genealogy itself bears within its carnal lowliness the perpetual testimony of the free divine initiative. This divine initiative is to brilliantly illuminate this genealogy from beginning to end. Abraham, its absolute beginning, is gratuitously chosen by God. He is perpetuated in a barren woman. The primogeniture is held not by Ismael but by Isaac. Later on it is not Esau who inherits it but Jacob, counter to what would have belonged to him *according to the flesh*. The same thing happens with Judah, who inherits instead of the first-born, as well as with David, who is the youngest of the brothers. In the long list are found not only just men but also great sinners.

Those who prided themselves on the purity of their Davidic origin, or who thought of Davidic in vain terms of racial purity, could not fail to note that in his genealogy Matthew introduced something most unusual: the names of four women, all of them foreigners and alien not only to their Jewish family but to the Jewish nation.

For instance, there is *Tamar*, the Canaanite, who, disguised as a harlot, obtains from her father-in-law the descendancy which belonged to her dead husband, according to levirate law, and which his relatives denied him. Then there is *Rahab*, also a Canaanite, thanks to whom the Jews can enter Jericho in the days of Joshua and who according to extra-biblical rabbinical tradition was the mother of Boaz, who in turns was the father of Obed whose mother was *Ruth* and whose grandfather was David. Ruth, too, was a foreigner and a member of a most hated people, the Moabites. Finally, there is *Bathsheba*, the adulteress, probably a Hittite as was her husband Uriah, whom David had sent into battle to be killed in order to have her. Later on she was no less than the mother of Solomon, the son of promise.

Where is there any room for racial pride, for pride in purity of blood, or in the merits of ancestors? Unpolluted blood, stainless justice, are not written in the lineage of the Messiah. On the contrary, if the Messiah is indebted to His ancestors, He is also indebted to foreigners and sinners, and even to those foreigners and sinners who have a claim to ancestry in regard to the Messiah.

Matthew is contented to point out the *genealogical logic* inscribed in the history of the Davidic lineage of the Messiah and thereby refute pride of flesh and worship of lineage. Those foreign women, to whom is due the perpetuation of the line of David, are the prefiguration of Mary: she, too, was alien to the line of David according to the flesh, and condemned by those who prided themselves on their genealogies. Yet, although eternally alien to the line of women who conceive through man, Mary is the mother of the new line of men who are born of God through faith.

7. Son of David and Son of God

Mary Virgin and *Mary, Spouse of Joseph*—these titles are not merely juxtaposed but are articulated and help to explain theologically how the Messianic title *Son of David* is to be understood. That the Messiah belongs to the line of David is not due to a bond of blood, for Joseph, Son of David, physically has no part in His conception. That the Messiah belongs to the house of David is due to an Alliance, a Matrimonial Alliance. A Matrimonial Alliance, however, which is also not explained by a mere human decision or choice, but by two assents of faith to the divine will. Consequently, it is at one and the same time a matrimonial alliance between two creatures, and an alliance of faith between two creatures and God.

The Messiah is the *Son of David* neither by the will nor the action of man nor by genealogy, but He enters into the genealogy by virtue of an assent of faith which *Joseph, Son of David*, gives to what is revealed to him as worked by God in Mary.

The Messiah is the *Son of God* neither by the will nor the action of man, but by virtue of an assent of faith which *Mary gives* to the working of the Spirit in her.

In order that the Messiah, Son of God and Son of David, should

1) come into the world and 2) in order that He should enter into the Davidic descendency, there were required two assents of faith: that of Mary and that of Joseph. Both assents found the true Israel, the true descendancy of Abraham, which is born, is propagated and perpetuated, not by human generation, but by faith.

Matthew emphasizes that the Davidic filiation of Jesus-Messiah is not a genealogical symbol that may be read, correctly understood and interpreted apart from faith. It is not a symbol which God had given in the domain of human generation, yielding to the carnality of the Jews who asked for signs in order to believe. It seems rather a contra-sign, for, prior to and independently of His incorporation into the line of David through the marriage of His Mother to a man of that line, the Messiah existed in events which Matthew does not evade; rather he shows how they are quite contrary to the messianic expectations of the Jews.

Matthew is very courageous and intellectually honest when he shoulders the task of expounding these seemingly incredible events. He does not soften them, he does not cover them up, confident they show such a coherence with the Old Testament that they will be acknowledged as most credible signs once the superficial crust of their apparent meaning has been penetrated.

Hence his recourse to the Old Testament, in constant parallel with the events, showing how it is not the prophecies which condemn Jesus-Messiah, but the true and concrete life of Jesus-Messiah which sheds light on the prophetic content of the Old Testament, and which extends their prophetic meaning to areas unsuspected by the common Jewish theological teachings of his times.

III

THE IMAGE OF MARY AS SEEN THROUGH ST. LUKE

Mary, Witness of Jesus Christ

1. *The purpose of Luke*

Luke the Evangelist's work consists of two books: his Gospel and the Acts of the Apostles. The first relates the history of Jesus, the second the history of the origins of the Church. The intent of the two is to illustrate the experience which the faithful of pagan origin encountered in the ecclesiastical community. This is done by explaining it in the light of its historical origins. How? By showing—in the present experience of the Holy Spirit descending on the ecclesial communities—the continuing action of that same Spirit which had operated in the Church of the Apostles, in the Life and Works of Jesus, and in the age-old prophecy of that same Spirit in the history of Israel.

Luke *is concerned* with the present and that is why he goes back to the past to explain it and interpret its religious significance. His written *work*, on the other hand, out of purely methodical reasons, starts out from the past and following a certain chronological order of events comes to the present. The prologue of his gospel shows us clearly that Luke has used the kinematographic technique of narrating:

"Many have undertaken to compile a narrative of the events which have been fulfilled in our midst, precisely as those events were transmitted to us by the original eye-witnesses and ministers of the word. I too have carefully traced the whole sequence of events from the beginning, and have decided to set it in writing for you, Theophilus, so that Your Excellency may see how reliable the instruction was that you received."

Luke is fully aware he is a secondary and late-coming *witness*. He is not an apostle, not an eyewitness of the origins of the Christian miracle. He joins the Church and is a relatively obscure and second-rank member. But he is not a Jew, and came to this new "sect," which was born of Judaism, with his Greek culture and mentality: well-instructed and fond of clarity and certainty, of order and of critical examination of events and witnesses.

In his prologue he clearly distinguishes 1) eyewitnesses (those who saw for themselves: *autoptai*) from the beginning (*ap'arjes*), who became ministers of this message and transmitted it (*pare-dosan*). They are the source of the tradition. 2) Others who devoted themselves to the task (*epejeiresan*: writing, putting the hand to) of repeating in writing and in the same order as the oral tradition, the accounts of witnesses (Mark, for instance?). They are those who set in writing these ancient traditions. 3) Finally, Luke himself who adopts his own order, an order which, founded on a diligent investigation of events, has as its end to reveal in these events their inner coherence and credibility.

From his actual (catechetical, apostolic) relationship with Theophilus—a real person or a personification of instructed pagans (as Luke himself had been), pagans who come to learn about the Christian faith—Luke undertakes his work which is at the same time both a history of the faith and a theology of history. As a good Greek historian, his work is based on eyewitnesses who are trustworthy.

His scrupulosity as an *historian* is reflected—among other things—in that he sets the events he relates in relation to certain coordinates or currents of history.

Theophilus was instructed in one of those communities of his day to which he and Luke belonged, in which he witnessed the working of the Spirit. Luke looks back and explains all that happens from the beginning as the work of the Holy Spirit. This centricity of the Holy Spirit in Luke's work is seen in the prologue of the Acts of the Apostles, the second book of his work:

> In my first account, Theophilus, I dealt with all that Jesus did and taught until the day he was taken up to heaven, having first instructed the apostles *he had chosen through the Holy Spirit.*

The Holy Spirit presided over and inspired the choice of the Apostles and is the divine bond between Jesus and the ecclesial Mission He begins.

Luke, in his writings addressed to non-Christian and Christian gentiles, cannot rest content with recourse to the Old Testament and proofs taken from Scripture. For those to whom they are addressed must view these elements integrated in a new and meaningful framework. Luke must be concerned about *solidity* and *certainty* and these elements must be proven, starting out from present, visible events in the Church. From these recent events he can go back to the biblical past, which of itself is of no interest to his pagan readers.

When Luke narrates the infancy of Jesus, he treats material of the distant past and he touches on the most remote part of his history. Luke could have left it out as did Mark and John. It was an especially thorny matter to explain to gentiles. As for Matthew, on the other hand, he could very easily show his Jewish readers how, through the events of Jesus' infancy, Scripture was fulfilled. However, those whom Luke addressed would not be convinced by arguments from Scripture unless they were presented as verified by the testimony of a witness, and as historically directed and clearly linked to the understanding of the present-day Church.

2. Mary as Witness

Mary is the witness of the infancy of Jesus, the witness mentioned above. We owe to Luke a list of Mary's traits, an enrichment of details of her image, which comes precisely from his interest in her as a privileged *witness* not only of Jesus' life but also of the theological meaning of that life.

If Luke's whole gospel is based on the testimony of eyewitnesses and if Luke dares to speak of the infancy of Jesus, it is because he relates it on Mary's testimony. Luke mentions twice in his account Mary's memories: "Mary treasured all these things in her heart" (2:19); "His mother meanwhile kept all these things in her heart" (2:51). These formulas recall how St. John in his gospel invokes his own testimony and also the analogous terms employed by Luke himself when he seems to refer to the testimony of neighbors and relatives:

> Fear descended on all in the neighborhood; throughout the hill country of Judea these happenings began to be recounted in the last detail. *All who heard stored these things up in their hearts*" (1:65-66).

> Her neighbors and relatives, *upon hearing* that the Lord had extended his mercy to her, rejoiced with her (1:58).

> The shepherds returned, glorifying God for all they had *heard and seen* (2:20).

Some of these testimonies, which Luke could only have obtained from other witnesses, must have come to him through Mary or from neighbors and relatives of Jesus, who—as we know—make up the primitive community and would preserve family traditions. But the ultimate source must have been Mary.

3. Mary's qualifications as a witness

Luke is very meticulous in bringing out Mary's qualifications as a witness. Mary is *full of grace*, the words of the Angel as we recite them in the Hail Mary! Mary is *instructed in Scripture*, as is gleaned from the biblical language of the Magnificat; as also from her profound biblical reflection on the events which are inseparably interwoven in Luke's narration and as is clear too from her levitic relationship with her cousin Elizabeth, who descended from the sacerdotal line of Aaron and was the wife of the priest Zechariah.

We pause here to emphasize this, because there are some who quite readily are inclined to attribute the accounts of Jesus' infancy to the imagination of the evangelists, as if they had freely invented them, inspired by the accounts of the infancy of great men of God, such as Moses and Samuel, which were found in the Old Testament.

It is undeniable that these accounts of Jesus' infancy are, as it were, a tapestry woven with threads of Old Testament reminiscences. Yet with what other thread could Mary have woven her meditation on the events, being a Jewish maiden, related to levites and priests, pious and filled with God, who assiduously and attentively attended the lectures and study groups of the synagogues? On opening up the coffer of his fondest memories, who can distinguish between what a cold historian might call events, a chronicle, and the representations, the personal interpretations, the emotional echoings in which, as in velvet, we wrap the jewels of our memory?

Luke knows he cannot ask Mary, his witness, to give testimony as an officially assigned witness. Nor is he in the least bit interested. For in the meditation by which Mary understood the events and remembers them, pondering on them in their midrashic interpretation, that is, in their predominant form of *haggadah* or narrative, there is something Luke appreciates more than chronicles on file. There is a revelation, made to a creature of supreme faith, of the meaning of the events of Jesus' infancy and childhood in the light of Scripture, and there is an illumination of obscure passages of Scripture in the light of the mysteries of the Savior's life. In this reciprocal illumining of present events by past ones, and of past events by present ones, there is not seen a method invented by Mary, but a very biblical procedure which reveals, without need of a signature, the true author: the Holy Spirit. As Luke likes to emphasize, it is the Holy Spirit who works in the Church, who worked in the life of Christ, through whose action Jesus was conceived in Mary, and who reveals Himself as the leader and guide of the entire history of salvation, not only (as in Matthew) from Abraham on, but from Adam himself, as Luke says in his genealogy of Jesus. It is the Holy Spirit who, through Mary, is giving witness to Jesus, and who began through her His task of teaching *all things* to the believers in Jesus Christ.

Therefore, Mary could not fail and does not fail in Luke's writing, not only at the moment of the infancy of Jesus, to be, as it were, the voice of a child not yet able to speak, but also in the infancy of the Church, when the Apostles, after the Ascension and while still behind locked doors for fear of the Jews, are constant in prayer—as Luke tells us at the beginning of the Acts of the Apostles—together with the Mother of Jesus, still without courage to speak, infant Apostles awaiting adulthood from the Holy Spirit.

This is why Mary discreetly disappears and humbly yields the word to her Son, when He—at the age of twelve, at His bar mitzvah, in the Temple of Jerusalem—becomes an adult teacher of the wisdom of His People, and capable of giving valid testimony of Himself and of the Father.

This is why Mary also disappears very soon from the Acts of the Apostles. Having become filled with the Holy Spirit on the day of Pentecost, the Apostles become Teachers of the New Law of the Spirit, servants of the Word, vested in might and power from on high, valid witnesses of the Passion and Resurrection, and of the fact that Jesus is the divine Messiah.

So Mary holds a very lowly post as a witness, and yields this post almost as soon as her provisory mission ceases to be indispensable. Yet her testimony remains as eternally valid and irreplaceable for that period of the conception and infancy and childhood of the Lord, at which she was present, and in the modest and obscure points which she knew how to read with faith, illumined by God, and before anyone else, as the fulfillment of the prophecies.

The content of Mary's testimony in the accounts of the infancy and childhood according to Luke, is polarized in the person of Jesus, the protagonist of the whole Gospel; around Him many figures move: Zechariah, Elizabeth, John the Baptist, Simeon and Anna the prophetess, the Doctors of the Temple, and Mary and Joseph.

4. *The fullness of the times*

Luke, a disciple of Paul, reflects in his work a very Pauline idea. It is an idea we have already seen in that passage from the Epistle to the Galatians which we quoted when treating Matthew: "But when the designated time had come, God sent forth his Son born of a woman" (Gal 4:4). The fullness of the times has come and it begins and consists of the life of Christ, for in Him is the center of the History of Salvation. .

The hidden life of the Lord's infancy and childhood is the critical dividing line where this fullness begins and antiquity ends. John the Baptist is the last personage of the Ancient Order. Jesus is the first of the New. Hence Luke parallels their miraculous conceptions, the angelic announcement to their parents, their symbolic names, revelatory of their respective identities and missions, their infancies and their growth. From this diptych of texts there stands out a certain similarity, but also the radical difference of both persons: John-precursor and Jesus-Messiah, John, the last prophet of the Old Order and Jesus the Son of God.

Luke takes pleasure in seeing, already from infancy, but even more, from before the Baptist's birth, his destiny to be the herald of the Messiah. The baby John leaps for joy in his mother's womb. She is filled with the Holy Spirit. It is the same Spirit to whose intervention is owed the miraculous fullness of the times

in Mary's womb. The Spirit who assures the continuity of one
and the same divine work throughout the discontinuity of the
times, of one that is extinguished and of one that is beginning.

5. A cloud of witnesses

Luke, the only evangelist who narrates to us the birth of
Jesus, assembles his witnesses around Jesus' cradle. All speak of
Him. Zechariah testifies by his very muteness. It is the negative
testimony of the muteness of the Old Law—of which he is a
priest—for explaining what is happening. God has no need of his
testimony or of his word for carrying on His work. It is in spite
of the muting of the Old Law, of the Ancient Liturgy, and the
Ancient Temple, of which Zechariah is a minister, that God
raises up a witness and a precursor: John the Baptist. While he—
also still mute leaps with joy in the womb of his mother—who
was sterile and advanced in years but now miraculously with
child, in order to bring forth the last fruit of ancient Israel—he
communicates to her the testimony about he who is to come:
"But who am I that the mother of my Lord should come to me?"
(1:43).

Elizabeth lends her voice to her son, still voiceless—as Mary
to hers—in order to become thus a precursor of the precursor,
a witness of Christ, and indirectly of Christ's mother, the precursor of Christ.

However, Mary is not a sole witness of the Lord who is
coming. We must keep this in mind when we consider Mary's
image according to St. Luke. In Luke's portrait, Mary is not
depicted isolated, a solitary figure, but in a group. It is by contrast, by reflection, by reflection of a family atmosphere, and a
contrasting personal genius, that her traits stand out. On one side,
Zechariah and Elizabeth. On another, Joseph and Mary. Over
there is the father of the one to whom the angelic message is
addressed, here is Mary, the Mother. Zechariah, unbelieving,
questions and is reduced to silence. Mary, full of faith, lifts her
voice in a transcendent assent.

In this group of witnesses Luke depicts for us, only Joseph is mute. Finally Zechariah receives his voice back to name the child—according to the mandate of the Angel—and to intone the Benedictus, testimony of the Davidic origin of Jesus and of the precursor mission of John. Elizabeth, Simeon and Anna are filled with the Holy Spirit and give testimony concerning the child. It is by reflection on and by contrast with all these voices that Luke presents the content of Mary's Magnificat, opening up a dimension of depth in her portrait, a window opening up not only the soul of her personality, but the interior, the heart which pondered all these things, guarding them zealously.

The eyes of the group of witnesses converge on Jesus, but the light which illumines their faces comes from the child. Thus with the light of His divinity, of which they speak to us, we see their faces shining and among them Mary's joyful face.

This is what so many painters have expressed so vividly in their canvasses, making the child the source of light which illumines the persons of the Nativity. Luke is their literary precursor.

6. Midrash

Luke takes up and employs a technique we might call *impressionist*. His literary style, especially in these accounts of the infancy, is replete with implicit references to the Old Testament, with allusions which are—each one—an evocation and suggestion of a world of ancient texts, called on also as witnesses. Is it not true that Jesus had, in His earthly life, invoked the testimony of the Scriptures? "Search the Scriptures in which you think you have eternal life—they also testify on my behalf" (Jn 5:39).

This meditative investigation into the Scriptures was not invented by Luke. It was used by the wise men of Israel, and of the one who practices it, the First Psalm says: "*Happy* the man . . . who delights in the law of the Lord and meditates on it night and day." It followed certain norms and is called Midrash. The Catholic Dictionary in the Jerusalem Bible defines it as: "The Hebrew word for examination, exposition, or explanation.

It is applied to the rabbinical exegesis of the Bible from the second to the tenth centuries . . ." Consequently it is not a free, mythological fabrication, but a serious reflection on Scripture of an inspirational and homiletic character. These are two types of Midrash. The first (*halakhah*) is a study of the sacred text to derive principles of conduct. The second (*haggadah*) is meditation on the narrative passages of Scripture to explain the salvific meaning in the Scriptural narration of an event.

Midrash is often a reflection which has as its object a problem or a new situation which arose in the course of the history of the people of God, to incorporate in Revelation a new fact, boldly prolonging the virtualities of Scripture.

But going beyond the bounds of study, Midrash touches on daily life in Israel. It becomes a proverbial style, which colors conversation, not only liturgical but also popular and domestic. There is a sanctifying purification of profane subjects by those which the Israelite hears in the synagogue sabbath after sabbath. It takes up and accommodates expressions from the text to fit situations of his life, and makes Scripture the vehicle and means of his communication. It creates an allusive, metaphorical indirect style that is quite unintelligible for one not conversant with Scripture. It is in this style of arcane allusions that Gabriel speaks to Mary, paraphrasing the text of a prophetical oracle found in Zephaniah.

Here are the parallel passages with the significant parts *italicized*:

> *Shout for joy, O daughter of Zion!* sing joyfully, O Israel! be glad and exult with all your heart, O daughter of Jerusalem! *The King of Israel is in your midst. Fear not, O Zion,* be not discouraged! *The Lord, your God is in your midst, a mighty Savior . . .*" (Zp 3:14-17).

> *Rejoice, O highly favored daughter! The Lord is with you . . .* "*Do not fear, Mary. You shall conceive and bear a son* and give him *the name Jesus* (Savior) . . . He will be called

Son of the Most High. The Lord God will give him *the throne of David* His father. He *will rule* over the house of Jacob forever" (Lk 1:28ff).

One of the common procedures of Midrash consists in describing a present (or future) event in the light of a past one, employing the same terms for pointing out similarities and comparing them. It is the procedure followed in the Book of Consolation (Deutero-Isaiah), which, when speaking about the return from exile, uses the terms of the liberation from Egypt (Exodus). God readies Himself to free His people once again.

The usage Gabriel makes in the Annunciation of the terms found in Zephaniah implies a twofold identification: Mary is identified with the Daughter of Zion, Jesus with Yahweh, King and Savior.

7. Mary, Daughter of Zion

Daughter of Zion (Bat Sion), is an expression which appears for the first time in the prophet Micah (1:13; 4:10ff). The term "Daughter" was commonly used in antiquity to refer to the population of a city. Daughter of Zion also designated the new section of Jerusalem, to the north of the city of David, where after the disaster of Samaria and before the fall of Jerusalem, the population of the North took refuge: the Remnant of Israel.

What is the meaning of its identification with Mary?

The Daughter of Zion, as a *theological expression*, means in Scripture the ideal and faithful Israel, the people of God in their most genuine and pure aspects. It may also be found to express occasionally definite groups of people, but it ever remains open to the future and to one person. Midrash is thereby capable of reflecting subtly the mysteries for which it is open, with special ability. Throughout the theological history of the expression *Daughter of Zion*, there has been a process from the part to the whole, which the angel now reverses, proceeding from the whole to a part, to one person, to Mary. The section of Jerusalem came to cover under its name the whole city, and the whole people, as bearers of a promise of salvation. Now it is a person, Mary, who is revealed as the Daughter of Zion par excellence, and the minute point of the cosmos, in which this magnificent promise is realized.

8. Mary and the Ark of the Covenant

Since we are primarily interested in Mary's image, we shall not detain ourselves long in showing how the second part of Gabriel's message, that which refers to Jesus, is a commentary also on the main text of the promise given to David (2 S 7), and alludes to other texts of the Bible which contain the brief message of the Angel, or the abbreviated form of that message. But, indeed, the parallel between Ex 40:35 and what the Angel announces to her about the mysterious manner of her conception is related to Mary. This parallel enables us to call on Mary piously and mystically in the Litany of Our Blessed Mother as *Foederis Arca*, the Ark of the Covenant, most appropriately, because over her, too, came the Cloud of God, within which He is present, acting on behalf of His People.

Here we have the parallel texts with the appropriate words *italicized*.

> *Then the cloud covered the meeting tent*, and *the glory* of the Lord filled the Dwelling . . . the cloud settled down upon it and the glory of the Lord filled the Dwelling" (Ex 40: 34-35).

> The Holy Spirit will come upon you and *the power of the Most High will overshadow you;* hence, *the holy offspring to be born will be called Son of God*" (Lk 1:35).

Mary's virginal conception is here described by way of the epiphany of God in the Ark of the Covenant. The cloud of God appears over both and its consequences are analogous. The Ark is filled with Glory; Mary is filled with the presence of a being who merits the name of Holy and of Son of God.

The action of the Holy Spirit, however, which manifests

itself as a shadowing cloud, is not limited to reposing on Mary. This manifestation is pointed out later on in Luke's gospel: the Baptism, the Transfiguration, texts in which the voice from heaven testifies to the Holiness and the divine Sonship of Jesus: "You are my beloved Son on whom my favor rests" (3:22), and "This is my Son, my Chosen One. Listen to him" (9:35).

We cannot detain ourselves here to unearth the midrashic allusions contained in St. Elizabeth's salutation to Mary, nor the anthological mosaic, likewise midrashic, of which the Magnificat is composed, a true testimony of Mary by Mary about herself.

9. The sign of the Spirit—Joy

In conclusion, I want to bring out an aspect of Mary's image according to Luke, one which transfigures the countenance of his privileged witness. Gabriel bids her: "Rejoice!", and in the Magnificat Mary "finds joy in God my Savior." Let us stay a while and gaze at Mary's face so filled with joy. Let us see it burst out into a canticle. Let us not linger on words which may distract us and waste our time on a curious biblical archeology. Let us contemplate the joy in the features Luke depicts for us.

This is the principal testimony Luke gives us. For in this primeval rejoicing he sees the source of the joy which flows in the Christian communities when they chant their faith in the Lord. Happy are they for having believed.

The only passage in the gospel which tells us about a thrill of joy in the Lord, is that in which Christ rejoices. Why? Because the Father has revealed Him to His believers. The incident is found in Matthew and in Luke. However, while Matthew confines himself to say soberly that Jesus "spoke thus," Luke says: "At that moment Jesus rejoiced in the Holy Spirit and said: 'I offer you praise, Father, Lord of heaven and earth, because what you have hidden from the learned and the clever you have revealed to the merest children. Yes, Father, *you have graciously willed it so*. Everything has been given over to me by the Father and no one knows the Son except the Father and no one knows the Father except the Son, and anyone to whom the Son wishes to reveal him' " (Lk 10:21-22; Mt 11:25-27).

Turning to his disciples he said to them *privately:* 'Blest are the eyes that see what you see. I tell you, many prophets and kings wished to see what you see but did not see it, and to hear what you hear but did not hear it' (Lk 10:23-24; Mt 13:16-17).

If anyone feels the joy of believing, if he rejoices and exults out of pure happiness because of his life of faith, let him know that this is an angelic voice within, and that he is hearing the language of angels. Let him know that this is the sheltering cloud of the Spirit over him and within him. It is the cloud of the Spirit and the Divine Presence in his inner life. It is the splendor of the manifestation of Glory, and the glorious manifestation of the divine Splendor. Let him know that *this* is the work of the Spirit in the Church. This is what will attract the illustrious Theophilus' attention. This is what Luke wants to explain to him, going back to its origin in Mary, in Jesus and in His disciples.

If anyone does not feel in himself this happiness, let him look at the face of Mary the believer lit up with joy, and let him hear the exultation of her Magnificat, and let himself be inspired and touched to the core by this joy. It is for Luke the guarantee of the solidity of the things Theophilus has heard.

IV

THE IMAGE OF MARY AS SEEN THROUGH ST. JOHN

The Echo of the Voice

A. *Two Enigmatic Facts*

1. *The first fact: John avoids calling her "Mary"*

The first fact we notice on reading St. John's Gospel, looking for what he says about Mary, is that he has avoided calling her by the name of "Mary." He never calls Jesus' Mother by this name and is the only one of the four evangelists who *systematically* avoids doing so. Mark uses her name, Mary, once. Matthew five times. Luke thirteen, twelve times in his Gospel and once in the Acts. John never uses it.

We say John *intentionally* avoids naming her as Mary, *because* there are indications that it is not a question of a casual but of a premeditated, intended and planned omission.

John does not ignore, for instance, the obscure name of Joseph which he mentions when he uses that phrase of incredulity which we commented on apropos of Mark and which in some form or other Matthew and Mark also use: "They kept saying: 'Is this not Jesus, the son of Joseph? Do we not know his father and mother? How can he claim to have come down from heaven?' " (Jn 6:42).

Secondly, John knows and frequently names in his gospel other women named "Mary": Mary of Cleopas, Mary Magdalene, Mary of Bethany, the sister of Lazarus and Martha. They are secondary persons in the Gospel and yet John does not avoid calling them by their own names. He does the same with other persons, whose names might apparently have been omitted without depriving the gospel of anything, such as Nicodemus and Joseph of Arimethea. If these names of less important figures have been kept for us, why is not Jesus' Mother mentioned by name? If, as some might suppose, it was because John did not want to repeat what other evangelists tell us, he would have been reluctant to give us the names of Joseph and the numerous Marys they have mentioned.

Thirdly, if there was a disciple who could and should know the Mother of Jesus, it surely was John, the disciple whom Jesus loved, and who in His last agony on the cross gave her to him as his own mother.

> Near the cross of Jesus there stood his mother, his mother's sister, Mary the wife of Cleopas, and Mary Magdalene. Seeing his mother there with the disciple whom he loved, Jesus said to his mother, 'Woman, there is your son.' In turn he said to the disciple, 'There is your mother.' From that hour onward, the disciple took her into his care (Jn 19:25-27).

And yet this is the disciple—who of all the others should be the last one to ignore the true name of the Mother of Jesus—who always alludes to her as the *Mother of Jesus* or, more briefly, *His Mother*, and avoids using her name, Mary, in his gospel. It is precisely this disciple, the one among all the others who had the greater right to refer to the Mother of Jesus as "My Mother," who insists on the title "Mother of Jesus" so exclusively that it has become a proper name.

John certainly knew Mary's name and *if as a matter of fact he does not use it*, he does so deliberately. It is not easy to detect his intention at first sight, but it is worth the effort to try to comprehend it.

2. *An hypothesis*

This hypothesis might explain why John omitted the name of Mary from his gospel. Perhaps he avoids using her name as a proper name for the Mother of Jesus because it seems to him too *common* for being applicable as a *proper name*. If the *proper* name is for us the one which distinguishes a person, an individual from all others; if, besides, to the Israelite mind the name reveals the essence of a person and expresses his or her mission in the history of salvation, then John had a reason for his practice. *Mary* is not a sufficiently proper name for designating in an adequate and unconfused manner the Mother of Jesus. It is a too *common* name for being her *proper* name. There are many Marys in the gospels, and doubtless there were very many among the people in Jesus' time, as there are still today among us. If John was looking for a unique name, a title that would indicate the unique destiny of that woman, a destiny never to be repeated, he chose well: *Mother of Jesus*. That is what she and she alone was, and is, for all ages.

Under this hypothesis, consequently, John, by not calling her Mary, and by always saying *Mother of Jesus, His Mother*, far from omitting the proper name of that woman, would be revealing to us her true name, the name which better expresses the very reason for her existence. However, let us try to go even further, and delve even more deeply into the possible hidden intentions of St. John.

3. *The second fact: Jesus' aloof conversations with Mary*

Let us analyze a second fact that comes to our attention as we study Mary's image as it emerges in the two unique passages of this gospel in which she appears: the Marriage Feast of Cana and the Crucifixion.

As we know, John, just as Mark, does not give us any account of Jesus' infancy. Furthermore, we must put aside the reference

His opponents make to His father and His mother, which John, like the synoptics, has preserved for us (Jn 6:42). We already saw, on treating Mark, what image of Mary this approach by the most ancient pre-evangelical tradition reveals. Therefore, we shall not insist on this aspect here, which is not proper to John.

The strictly Johannine material about the Mother of Jesus—unfortunately for our pious curiosity, but fortunately for one considering it briefly as we do— is reduced to these two scenes which together cover but 14 verses: The Marriage Feast of Cana, (Jn 2:1-11) and the Crucifixion (Jn 19:25-27). If it were not for John we would not know that Jesus had assisted, with His Mother and His disciples, at the marriage feast. Nor would we know that the Mother of Jesus followed His Passion closely, and was one of the few who were found at the foot of the Cross.

Now, here is the second fact we are to consider. Among all the passages in the gospels about Mary, there are very few which preserve for us what seems to be a conversation between Jesus and Mary, His Mother. To be exact there are three: two in John's gospel and one in Luke about Jesus lost and found in the Temple when His grieving Mother reproached Him in these words: "Son, why have you done this to us? You see that your father and I have been searching for you in sorrow" (Lk 2:48). Jesus answers in those enigmatic words, which are the first words spoken by Jesus in Luke: "Why did you search for me? Did you not know I had to be in my Father's house?" (Lk 2:29).

One who reads the Johannine dialogues after having received this first impression from Luke cannot help but feel more disconcerted. In the Marriage Feast of Cana, Jesus replies to His Mother who tells Him about the shortage of wine: "*Woman, how does this concern of yours involve me? My hour has not yet come.*" In the crucifixion scene: "*Woman, there is your son.*"

Let us note, then, that in the three dialogues we have, Jesus seems to place an austere distance between Himself and His Mother. These are precisely the passages which, by presenting Jesus and Mary in a face-to-face, informal conversation, should have appropriately reflected the tenderness and affection that undoubtedly united these two beings on earth. Yet they are the very passages which, on the contrary, present us with an apparently austere image of this relationship, capable of scandalizing our contemporaries: 1) "Woman, *how does this concern of yours involve me?*" 2) "Woman, *there is your son.*"

John seems to have taken up and underlined what Luke anticipated in his scene. The Mother of Jesus only appears in his gospel in these two scenes of a dialogue, and Jesus appears in them to be distant toward His Mother: 1) by a question which questions her relationship; 2) by interpreting it with the generic and even cold "Woman"; 3) by handing her over to another as her son.

The impression, as we said, is disconcerting, and adds a second fact, which needs to be explained, to the already enigmatic silence about the name of the Mother of Jesus.

B. *Explanations*

Let us attempt to give an explanation of these two enigmatic facts.

1. *"Do whatever he tells you"*

St. John's Gospel stresses God's revelation in Jesus Christ as the revelation of the *Father of Jesus.* God is the Father of Jesus. John is the evangelist who shows us best the intimacy of Jesus with His Father; the current of mutual love and benevolence which unites them; how Jesus lives and dies for doing that which pleases His Father; how He nourishes Himself on paternal benevolence, and how it is His true life: "The Father loves me for this: that I lay down my life to take it up again. No one takes it from me; I lay it down freely. I have power to lay it down, and I have power to take it up again. This command I received from my Father" (Jn 10:17-18). "The Father and I are one" (Jn 10:30). "Whoever has seen me has seen the Father" (Jn 14:9).

It is as a parallel and by analogy with these terms found throughout St. John: *my Father, the Father of Jesus,* that I think we must understand John's insistence on referring to Mary alone and exclusively as: *His Mother, the Mother of Jesus.*

Just as God is for Jesus *the Father,* omnipresent in His life and ever on His lips: My Father, the Father who sent Me, I go to the Father, My Father and your Father, the Father who loves Me, the house of My Father . . . so too and in order to point out a mystical analogy, in order to emphasize a parallel spiritual reality, John calls her who is, as it were, an echo of the divine Paternal Figure—not only through a physical maternity, but also and principally through a communion in the same Holy Spirit— the Mother of Jesus.

One of the principal aims of the scene at Cana seems to us to be—as John intended—to show to what extent the *Mother of Jesus* is one in her spirit with the Spirit of the *Father of Jesus.*

In fact, at the scene at Cana, it would appear that John desires to emphasize the coincidence of the veiled testimony Mary gives Jesus before men with the testimony His Father gives Jesus: "Do whatever he tells you," says the Mother. "Listen to him," says the Father, both meaning: Obey him. Indeed, we know through the testimony of the synoptics, that in the two decisive moments of the Baptism and of the Transfiguration, the heavens open over Jesus, and a Voice comes down—the Voice of God—which proclaims (with slight variations according to each evangelist): "This is my beloved Son, in whom I am well pleased."

At the *Baptism* the motive of this voice—which is revealed as that of the Father—is a testimonial that Jesus is the Messiah and the Son of God, a testimonial which is a solemn declaration of the public beginning of his mission as Son of God and His destiny as Messiah. In the *Transfiguration* the motive of this voice is to give confirmation and a guarantee of Messianic authenticity to the *Via dolorosa* which Jesus announces to His disciples. The celestial voice completes its message: "This is my

Son, my Chosen One" with the command: "Listen to him."

St. John is the only evangelist who does not relate the scene of the Baptism. Nor does he make any reference to the heavenly voice which—according to the synoptics—let itself be heard at the Baptism. In its stead, he gives not only a more profound and explicit testimony of the Baptist, but also—it seems to us—of Mary's voice: "Do whatever he tells you," which is equivalent to the "Listen to him" of the divine Voice in the Transfiguration, but prior to it at the beginning of Jesus' ministry.

Before the scene at Cana, there is no record of Jesus mentioning His Father by name, not even once. The first time will be at the scene of the cleansing of the Temple, which comes immediately after that of Cana. It is through His Mother that there comes to Jesus before the cleansing of the Temple, as through a most faithful echo, the Voice of His Father. Not, as in the synoptics, through a voice from the heavens, or as further on in John's Gospel as a thunder clap—the by-standers, to whom it is addressed, differ as to whether it is thunder or the voice of an angel—but as the simple words of a woman whose prophetic character only Jesus could know, hidden as it was under the most modest garb of everyday language.

A proof that Jesus recognized in His Mother's words an echo of His Father's Voice, is that although He has told her: "My hour has not yet come," when she says to the waiters: "Do whatever he tells you," He changes His mind and changes the water into wine.

Jesus did so not out of mere deference or courtesy, and much less out of weakness, yielding to an inopportune request. It was an acknowledgment in His Mother's voice, of the clearest Echo of His Father's will. Obeying this voice, Jesus "revealed his glory, and his disciples believed in him." St. John is careful in other passages of the gospel to stress Jesus' great care not to do anything save what the Father commands, showing only that which His Father has shown Him and zealously guarding what His Father gives Him.

If, then, Mary is on the one hand, *Daughter of Zion* in as much as she embodies the holiest of the People of God, she is also *Daughter of the Voice*, which is the Hebrew term for what we call echo. Echo of the Voice of God—*Bat Kol*, Daughter of the Voice.

2. *Between Cana and Calvary*

We cannot judge the importance John's gospel gives to the image of Mary from the number of references made to her for, as we have seen, there are but few. We have to judge its importance from the significant setting, within the whole scheme of the gospel, of the two sole and brief scenes in which she appears: Cana and Calvary. This we do not only, of course, from its place in the text, but also from its revealing content.

Cana and Calvary form a magnificent Marian setting in John's gospel. They set the whole public life of Jesus, as it were, in parentheses. They place between Marian quotation marks, as it were, the mission of Jesus. They embrace, as it were, in maternal love—very prudent but at the same time revealing a full comprehension and compenetration between Mother and Son—the whole public life of Jesus from its inauguration at Cana to its consummation on Calvary.

The Mary of St. John is not only—as in Mark—the Mother sharing in the contempt shown her Son. Nor is she—as in Mark and Luke—a fleeting star which illumines the obscure origin of the Messiah or the night of an infancy lost in the forgetfulness of men.

The Mother of Jesus is for St. John the witness and the principal actor in the very life of Jesus. Her presence at the beginning and at the end, at the prelude and denouement, is like the sudden, fleeting, but illuminating eruption of a flash of lightning, and comparable also to the double, unexpected thunder of the Voice of the Father, at the Baptism and at the Transfiguration.

3. *The conversation at Cana*

The Mother of Jesus, such as John presents her to us, is knowing and understanding. She is a worthy and intelligent conversationalist. As one who is initiated into the mystery of the hour of Jesus, she communicates with Him in a language of veiled allusions to a common secret.

One who overhears this language may well get a false impression from the apparent banality of the Mother's intervention: "They have no more wine," and the apparent aloofness and cold discourtesy of the Son: "Woman, how does this concern of yours involve me? My hour has not yet come."

It is on the occasion of a wedding feast that Mother and Son in their conversation touch on the theme of the Covenant. The Old and the New. Old wine and new wine. Ordinary wine and excellent wine which is a water of ritual purifications, which flows from the rock of unbelief and only washes the exterior. A New Covenant which gushes forth inexplicably by force of the words of Christ, as good wine, as blood flowing from His Heart through His open side, and gives joy from within.

The Mother's remark: "They have no wine," has within it a discreet midrashic allusion to the joy of the Messianic Covenant yet to come, and of which wine is a symbol in Scripture.

We know through St. Luke that not only Jesus, but also Mary, speaks and understands this midrashic style, which interweaves Scripture and ordinary life. In John's gospel, Jesus appears as the Master teaching in this style, which is based on material realities and makes them into proverbs filled with divine meaning: *He spoke of the Temple...of His Body; as the wind... is everyone who is born of the Spirit; He who drinks of this water will thirst again but he who drinks of the water I will give him . . . ; my flesh is food indeed . . .*

And if Mary's remark about the shortage of wine is to be understood as the nucleus of a much wider dialogue, which St. John abbreviates and reproduces only in its essence, the obscure response of Jesus is to be interpreted, not as that of someone who is teaching someone ignorant, but as that of one who is responding to an intelligent question.

The words of Jesus: *"Woman, how does this concern of yours involve me? My hour has not yet come,"* rather than denying a relationship with Mary, is an advanced reference to what—once the hour of Jesus has arrived—will create between Him and His Mother the perfect bond, ultimate and definitive, before which those already strong bonds which unite Him with His Mother in the flesh and in the Spirit will fade away. It will be a bond so strong that—as we shall see—it will be possible to say that *the hour of Jesus* is at the same time *the hour of Mary*, the hour of an eschatological enlightenment, in which the Crucified shows to her in John the son of her sorrows, the first-born of the Church.

If the Mother indirectly asks about the *joy* symbolized by the wine (*There is no feast if there is no wine*, says the Jewish proverb), Jesus alludes to a joy which comes in the sorrow of His hour, of His Passion, a joy which Jesus will opportunely announce to His Mother from the Cross, as the sorrowful joy of enlightenment.

4. *The scene on Calvary*

With this we have begun our response to the second surprising fact: that of the coldness and indifference Jesus seemingly displays in His conversations with His Mother. Yet, at the same time, we have just insinuated the meaning of the second Marian scene in the Gospel of St. John: that of Calvary. Let us consider it more attentively:

Near the cross of Jesus stood his Mother, his mother's sister, Mary the wife of Cleopas, and Mary Magdalene. Seeing his mother there with the disciple whom he loved, Jesus said to his mother, 'Woman, there is your son.' In turn he said to the disciple, 'There is your mother.' From that hour onward, the disciple took her into his care (19:25-27).

For interpreting this passage, we think we can start out from the words *from that hour onwards*. John likes to use words which are apparently common, but which are full of meaning. These words are an example. This is so because *that hour* is nothing less than the hour of Jesus. Of that hour Jesus said: *"The hour has come . . . , yet what should I say? Father save me from this hour! But it was for this that I came to this hour. Father glorify your name!"* (Jn 12:23-27).

For St. John, the hour of someone is the time when he accomplished the task for which he was particularly destined. The hour of the unbelieving Jews is the time when God permits them to perpetrate the crime in the person of Christ or of His disciples:

Yes, *the hour* is coming for everyone who kills you to think that he is offering worship to God. And these things they will do because they have not known the Father nor me. But these things I have spoken to you, that when the time has come you may remember that I told you" (Jn 16:3-4) (Douay version).

This expression *the hour* possibly goes back to Jesus Himself. Apart from the numerous passages of St. John, Luke also hands down to us a passage in which the Lord speaks of His Passion as *the hour:* "But this is your hour—the triumph of darkness!" (Lk 22:53).

The hour of Jesus is that moment when there is accomplished the task for which He was sent into this world by the Father. It is the hour of His victory over Satan, over sin, and over death: "Now (at this hour) has judgment come upon this world, now will this world's prince be driven out, and I—once I am lifted up from earth—will draw all men to myself" (Jn 12:31-32).

Since it is the hour of the Passion, a sorrowful but triumphant hour at the same time, it is for St. John intimately united to glory, the glorious triumph of Jesus. This glory is manifested for the first time at Cana. The glory of Cana is the same as that with which the Father will glorify His Son on the Cross. Mary is the witness of this glory in both scenes.

This co-existence of suffering and glory which there is in
this hour, is particularly well expressed in a comparison Jesus
makes at the Last Supper and which compares His hour with
that of a woman giving birth to a child:

> A woman about to give birth has sorrow, because *her hour*
> has come. But when she has brought forth the child, she no
> longer remembers the anguish for her joy that a man is born
> into the world" (Jn 16:21) (Douay).

I think that this comparison did not come to Jesus' mind
casually on the eve of His passion. Rather I believe it is, as it
were, an anticipatory explanation of the scene on which we are
meditating and that, in the light of this explanation, John would
have comprehended the depth of the gesture and of the last
words of Jesus in His agony to him and to Mary. Did Jesus,
John and Mary recall the prophet oracle of Jeremiah, or of some
other prophet?

> Yes, I hear the moaning, as of a woman in travail, like the
> anguish of a mother with her first child—the cry of a daughter
> of Zion gasping, as she stretches forth her hands: 'Ah, woe
> is me! I sink exhausted before the slayers!' (Jr 4:31).

At the foot of the Cross, the Daughter of Zion moans and
feels her soul sink exhausted before the slayers of her Son. Jesus,
who sees her thus in anguish like a mother bearing her first child,
aware of the breaking of her heart, alluding perhaps in a veiled
manner to some prophetical oracle such as that of Jeremiah,
consoles her with the greatest consolation that can possibly be
given to one who has just given birth to a child. He shows her
that child saying: "Here is your son" and points to *the disciple*,
the first-born of the Church, of the People of God, whom Jesus
has acquired by His blood, blessed John who has stayed at the
gates of Wisdom in that hour of darkness:

> Happy the man watching daily at my gates, waiting at my
> doorposts (Pr 8:34).

John, the first-born of the Church, stays close to the doorposts of the gate of Wisdom, stained with the blood of the Lamb, in order to be safe from the passing of the exterminating Angel.

Here we have pointed out where we must go in order to find the explanation of the term *woman* Jesus uses when He addresses His Mother in the gospel of John. Both at Cana and on Calvary Jesus sees in her something more than the woman who gave Him His mortal body and to whom He is united by personal, casual bonds of affection.

For Jesus, Mary is the *Woman*, whom the Book of Revelation describes in mythological terms, in the pains of childbirth, pursued by the dragon, fleeing into the desert with her first-born. She is the woman in Jeremiah bringing forth her first-born among assassins. Jesus does not see His Mother—as we see ours—in a pious but exclusive and narrow view, but in the perspective of the hour, fixed by the Father beforehand, in which He would receive and give glory. This glory that is a current which comes and goes, and, as Jesus says, is in those who believe in Him: "For these I pray . . . these you have given me, for they are really yours, just as all that belongs to me is yours . . . It is in them that I have been glorified" (Jn 17:9-10). The Father glorifies His Son *in* His disciples, called to be one with Him, as He and the Father are one. Mary, the Mother of He who is one with the Father, is also the Mother of those who by faith are one with the Son.

Therefore, when Jesus from His Cross, where stood His Mother, designated John as her son, He designated Himself. He assigns her to His own care, not as she sees Him crucified in His Hour, but as she must see Him glorified in His own, in whom the Father assigns her to herself, not under her appearance of a Mother deprived of her son, the humiliated Mother of a condemned criminal, but also according to her reality: first born of her true Son, born in the corporeal stature—initially, it is true, but now perfected—of Son of Man.

V

CONCLUSION

Here we have come to the end of our meditations on the image of Mary seen through the four evangelists. It is clear that all of them speak of Mary with the ultimate intention of saying what they desire about Jesus. Their discourses on Christ find light and support in her. No one could prescind from her by speaking of Jesus and by presenting what they do say as the Gospel, that is, as the announcement of salvation.

Mary is not the Gospel. There is no Gospel of Mary. But, without Mary, neither is there any Gospel. So she is not missing from any of the four.

She is not only needed for wrapping Jesus in swaddling clothes (and for washing them . . .). She is not only necessary for teaching Him to take His first steps, toddling in our world of men. Her mission is not only co-extensive with that of the earthly Jesus, but goes far beyond His death on the Cross: she is present at His resurrection and the rise of His Church.

Garbed with the sun, crowned with stars, standing on the moon, Mary, as her Son, remains forever. Although the world and the stars wear out as an old garment, to the confusion of those who put their security and vainglory in these things, Mary will go on forever, as the Word of God of which she is the Echo.

Mary, the Mother of Jesus, belongs to the store of goods common to Jesus and His disciples. His Father is our Father. His hour is our hour, His glory, our glory. His Mother, our Mother.

BIBLIOGRAPHY

1. MONOGRAPHS

ALDAMA DE, José A.: *Maria en la Patrística de los siglos I y II*, Madrid, BAC, 1970 (Vol. 300).

GALOT, Jean: *María en el Evangelio*, Madrid, Apostolado de la Prensa, 1960.

MORI, Edios G.: *Figlia di Sion e Serva di Yavé*, Bologna, Ed. Dehoniana, 1969.

MULLER, Alois: *Puesto de Maria y su cooperación en el Acontecimiento Cristo* en: *Mysterium Salutis*, Vol. III, T. II, pp. 405-528, Madrid, Ed. Cristiandad, 1971.

VERGES, Salvador: *María en el Misterio de Cristo*, Salamanca, Ed. Sígueme, 1972 (Col. Lux Mundi 31).

2. THE GOSPELS

A) The Four Gospels

CABA, José: *De los Evangelios al Jesús Histórico*, Madrid, BAC, 1971 (Vol. 316).

McHUGH, John: *The Mother of Jesus in the New Testament*, Garden City, N. Y., Doubleday, 1975.

SCHNACKENBURG, Rudolf: *Cristologia del Nuevo Testamento* en: *Mysterium Salutis*, Vol. III, T. I, pp. 245-416, Madrid, Ed. Cristiandad, 1971).

VAWTER, Bruce: *Introducción a los cuatro evangelios*, Santander, Ed. Sal Terrae, 1969 (Col. Palabra Inspirada 9).

B) Synoptics

TROADEC, Henry: *Comentario a los Evangelios Sinópticos*, Madrid, Fax, 1972 (Col. Actualidad Bíblica 17).

C) Mark

MANSON, T. W.: *The Sayings of Jesus*, London, SCM Press, 1949¹-1964.

Jesus the Messiah, London, Hodder and Stoughton, 1943¹-1961.

D) Matthew

BOVER, José M.: *Un texto de san Pablo (Gál 4, 4-5) interpretado por san Ireneo*. Estudios Eclesiásticos 17 (1943), 145-181.

DANIEL-ROPS: *La vida cotidiana en Palestina en tiempo de Jesús*, Buenos Aires, Hachette, 1961 (Nueva Col. Clío).

FORD, J. M.: *Mary's Virginitas Post-Partum and Jewish Law*, Biblica 54 (1973), 269-272.

FRANKEMOLLE, Hubert: *Jahwehund und Kirche Christi*, Múnster, Aschendorf, 1974 (Neutestamentliche Abhandlungen, N.F. 10).

GUTZWILLER, Richard: *Jesus der Messias. Christus im MatthäusEvangelium*, Einsiedeln-Köln-Zürich, Benziger Verlag, 1949.

JEREMIAS, Joachim: *Jérusalem au Temps de Jésus*, París, Du Cerf, 1967.

E) Luke

BORREMANS, John: *L'Esprit Saint dans la catéchèse évangelique de Luc*, Lumen Vitae 25 (1970), 103-122.

BURROWS, Eric: *The Gospel of the Infancy*, London, Burns y Oates y Washbourne, 1940 (Col. The Bellarmine Series 6).

LAURENTIN, René: *Structure et Théologie de Luc I-II* Paris, Gabalda, 1964 (Col. Etudes Bibliques) (*). *Marie en Luc 2, 48-50*, Paris, Gabalda, 1966 (Col. Etudes Bibliques).

F) John

BRAUN, F. M.: *Jean le Théologien*, Vol. III: *Sa Théologie*, T. I: *Le Mystère de Jésus-Christ*, Paris, Gabalda, 1966 (Col. Etudes Bibliques).

DE LA POTTERIE, Ignace: *Das Wort Jesu 'Siehe deine Mutter' und die Annahme der Mutter durch den Jünger (Joh 19, 27b)* en: *Neues Testament und Kirche* (Festschrift f. Rudolf Schnackenburg), Freiburg-Basel-Wien, Herder, 1974, pp. 191-219.

FEUILLET, André: *L'Heure de Jésus et le Signe de Cana*, Ephemerides Theol. Lovanienses 36 (1960). 5-22.

LEROY, Herbert: *Rätsel und Missverständniss*, Tübingen, Dis. doctoral, Ed, del Autor, 1967.